Preface

There are many introductory books on tl
is not one of them. While this book has brief explanations of
main concepts, it is intended for people who have already read
about and understood the Law of Attraction and the power of
manifestation in depth, and want to put it into practice
effectively. This is a workbook, an application manual, a
traveler's companion, whatever you want to call it, it is meant to
help the reader in the application of what was already learned.

Introduction

You want to improve. Just the fact that you hold this book in
your hands shows that you are serious about achieving what
you desire in life. You know you want better. This book will help
you to first decide what you want in life and what you want
from life. Manifestation is the merging of belief, vision, and
action; a powerful tool at your disposal when used responsibly,
despite most people being oblivious to this power. Most people
don't know what they want in life or are very vague about it.
One needs goals to know what they are moving towards. It is
very important to be specific so that the subconscious can also
help in achieving these goals. Without goals, one is like a feather
in the wind or a ship without a rudder, tossed about to and fro
by the winds and the waves of randomness. Another important
reason people cannot accomplish what they want in life is
because they operate in the wrong frequency.

There really are positive and negative vibrations dominating our moods, our relationships, our lives. Like so many notes coming together to create a symphony, except the string section is playing in the wrong key. Negative thoughts, anxiety, and worry create disorder and chaos, that slowly eats away at a person's soul. One more reason why people do not get what they want in life is because they consume too much information about manifestation or the Law of Attraction, without applying what was learned. They just don't know where to start due to information overload — that is where this book comes in. It contains enough techniques and modalities to manifest goals and live a more successful, positive life. The approach in this book is developed to help you achieve your goals, big and small. The manifestation exercises in this book are to be filled with personal content; make use of the techniques and concepts so that you, too, can achieve fulfillment on a higher level. You might know some of the exercises while others may be new to you. I have nevertheless included an explanation as to why they are important. You are free to start with any exercise or technique you wish, each being independent of the other yet serving the same purpose — to make you the best version of yourself, by achieving the goals you hold dear in life, through positive manifestation. A tool is only as beneficial as it is used. Use this new tool of yours to the maximum to receive maximum benefit. Eliminate excuses. You, alone, are responsible for your success and happiness. Now is your time to start manifesting and enjoy life!

Fully Yours

Agrim

This journal belongs to

Agrim Ranganathan

ISBN: 9781676364184

The Vision Board

One thing that cannot be overstated is the purpose of a vision board. A constant reminder of our purpose, it keeps our goals and dreams right in front of us, giving us hope. It is usually in the shape of a poster, where cut out pictures of personal goals are pasted, similar to a picture collage. There could be a picture of your dream car or house, an expensive watch, or a vacation destination. Seeing those pictures, imagining and intensely feeling what it feels like to be, to do, and to have your goals is essential in manifestation. You can paste pictures from magazines, draw your own, or just write down the names of those things you wish to manifest. It should be loud and eye catching, though. It should catch your vision and bring your thoughts back to what is important — improving you. When distractions pile up, it is easy to lose sight of the prize. When you lose sight, you get lost. The vision board is like a lighthouse on a foggy night. As well as having one on your wall, adding a vision board to this book brings the advantage that you can take your "lighthouse" with you anywhere you go. This book should be filled in daily but before getting to the exercises, look at your vision board as soon as you open this book, it will reset your bearings and prompt inspiration. There are two double pages dedicated to your vision board so you have enough room to add as much as you want.

Dream big. If your dreams don't scare you, you're not dreaming big enough.

You could use one double page for work related goals and the other double page for personal goals.

Personal Life

Professional Life

Where do you see yourself in one year?

_____

_____

_____

_____

_____

_____

_____

_____

Where do you see yourself in five years?

_____

_____

_____

_____

_____

_____

_____

_____

_____

What do you want?

Write everything that comes to your mind.

What do you want exactly?

Be very specific in terms of color, appearance, size...

_____

_____

_____

_____

_____

_____

_____

_____

_____

_____

_____

_____

_____

_____

_____

_____

_____

_____

_____

_____

_____

What do you have? (future perspective)

Write in present tense as if all you wanted already happened.
How do you feel? How is it to drive your dream car for example,
or to be in your dream home with your dream partner. Visualize
while you write everything down.

_____

_____

_____

_____

_____

_____

_____

_____

_____

_____

_____

_____

_____

_____

_____

_____

_____

_____

5 x 55

Now turn the goal you want to manifest into a tangible sentence. Short and sweet. During the next 5 days write it down 55 times each day. Focus on one thing and one thing alone, being very specific. Form a precise sentence and use present tense. If you want to manifest a certain job, for example, you could write the following sentence: My new job at XYZ brings me joy and happiness and pays me $--- per month. The sentence is like an affirmation that you repeat 55 times a day.

Why 5 and 55?

Just as it was determined that 10,000 hours of practice and performing a certain skill makes one an expert in that skill, so too was it determined that 5 and 55 are the right amounts needed to stick. Learning from the experience of others saves us the pain of arduous discovery. As an aside for those who are interested, in numerology the number 5 indicates change, realignment, and transformation. Whereas the angel number 55 stands for personal strength and self-determination. Remember, the sentence or affirmation should be short. Go with something constructive and positive at first glance. Always phrase the sentence in present tense and include words that express your gratitude. Ask yourself: What is the most important thing for me right now? What would I like to manifest in the very near future? Phrase your sentence now and write it down 55 times a day for the next 5 days.

Day 1

Date:

1.

2.

3.

4.

5.

6.

7.

8.

9.

10.

11.

12.

13.

14.

15.

16.

17.

18.

19.

20.

21.

22.

23.

24.

25.

26.

27.

28.

29.

30.

31.

32.

33.

34.

35.

36.

37.

38.

39.

40.

41.

42.

43.

44.

45.

46.

47.

48.

49.

50.

51.

52. _____

53. _____

54. _____

55. _____

_____

Day 2   Date:

1. _____

2. _____

3. _____

4. _____

5. _____

6. _____

7. _____

_____

8.

9.

10.

11.

12.

13.

14.

15.

16.

17.

18.

19.

20.

21.

22.

23.

24.

25.

26.

27.

28.

29.

30.

31.

32.

33.

34.

35.

36.

37.

38.

39.

40.

41.

42.

43.

44.

45.

46.

47.

48.

49.

50.

51.

52.

53.

54.

55.

Day 3   Date:

1.

2.

3.

4.

5.

6.

7.

8.

9.

10.

11.

12.

13.

14.

15.

16.

17.

18.

19.

20.

21.

22.

23.

24.

25.

26.

27.

28.

29.

30.

31.

32.

33.

34.

35.

36.

37.

38.

39.

40.

41.

42.

43.

44.

45.

46.

47.

48.

49.

50.

51.

52.

53.

54.

55.

Day 4   Date:

1.

2.

3.

4.

5.

6.

7.

8.

9.

10.

11.

12.

13.

14.

15.

16.

17.

18.

19.

20.

21.

22.

23.

24.

25.

26.

27.

28.

29.

30.

31.

32.

33.

34.

35.

36.

37.

38.

39.

40.

41.

42.

43.

44.

45.

46.

47.

48.

49.

50.

51.

52.

53.

54.

55.

Day 5   Date:

1.

2.

3.

4.

5.

6.

7.

8.

9.

10.

11.

12.

13.

14.

15.

16.

17.

18.

19.

20.

21.

22.

23.

24.

25.

26.

27.

28.

29.

30.

31.

32.

33.

34.

35.

36.

37.

38.

39.

40.

41.

42.

43.

44.

45.

46.

47.

48.

49.

50.

51.

52.

53.

54.

55.

Your Cheques

In the now famous anecdote, actor Jim Carrey wrote himself a check for ten million dollars for "acting services rendered".

This is an act of visualization materialized. This is a great leap.

The then unknown Carrey chose a date in the future to work towards, using the power of manifestation. He kept the check in his wallet and looked at it regularly, visualizing what it would be like to have ten million dollars. It was a constant reminder of his goal. With the hard work that should follow visualization, Carrey's acting career took off and, indeed, by the year of the post dated check he was so famous that he signed a contract for his next movie with a big payout. That role was for the movie "Dumb and Dumber," for which he received ten million dollars for 'acting services rendered.'

How about writing yourself some checks? Carry them with you and visualize that you have already manifested the amounts of money.

How to fill out your check - Example

Front

BANK OF ABUNDANCE   1111
Date 2 0 2 7 1 0 0 1
Y Y Y Y MM DD
Pay to the Order of _Cassandra Williams_ $ 2.500.00
two thousand five hundred / 100 Dollars
Abundance Memo _Royalty Earnings in September 2027_ Per _The Universe_
8888   11118   123   123   456 8

Back

Manifested on: _October 1st 2027_

APPROVED

Signature or Stamp

I am so happy and grateful because money is coming to me from various sources on a continuous basis.

Check no. 1111 used to manifest:

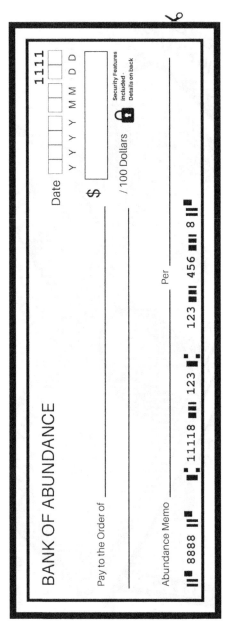

BANK OF ABUNDANCE

1111

Date

Y Y Y Y M M D D

Pay to the Order of

$

/ 100 Dollars

Security Features
included ·
Details on back

Abundance Memo _____ Per _____

⑁

⑈ 8888 ⑈⑈ ⑆ 11118 ⑈⑈⑈ 123 ⑆⑆ 123 ⑈⑈⑈ 456 ⑈⑈⑈ 8 ⑈⑈

For manifesting purposes only.

Manifested on: _____

Signature or Stamp

I am so happy and grateful because money is coming to me from various sources on a continuous basis.

For manifesting purposes only.

Check no. 1112 used to manifest:

BANK OF ABUNDANCE

Date

1112

Y Y Y Y   M M   D D

Pay to the Order of _____

£ _____

_____ / 100 Pounds

🔒 Security Features
included .
Details on back

Abundance Memo _____ Per _____

||" 8888 ||•"   •:" 11118 ■■I 123 ||:   123 ■■I 456 ■■I 8 ||•"

For manifesting purposes only.

Manifested on: _____

Signature or Stamp

I am so happy and grateful because money is coming to me from various sources on a continuous basis.

For manifesting purposes only.

Check no. 1113 used to manifest:

BANK OF ABUNDANCE

1113

Date
Y Y Y Y   M M   D D

Pay to the Order of

€

/ 100 Euros

Security Features
included -
Details on back

Per

Abundance Memo

⑊ 8888 ⑊   ⑊ 11118 ⑊ 123 ⑊   123 ⑊ 456 ⑊ 8 ⑊

For manifesting purposes only.

Manifested on: _____

Signature or Stamp

I am so happy and grateful because money is coming to me from various sources on a continuous basis.

For manifesting purposes only.

Positive Affirmations

Positive affirmations are a way of tapping into the subconscious mind, making incremental improvements in the negative self-talk cycle — which has a lot to do with society's endless chatter of telling us who we are "supposed" to be. Repeating these affirmations earnestly and often will eliminate limiting beliefs and actually change the way you think. Remember to say them with full conviction and feel the flood of optimism.

I am

Eliminate Negativity

Roads are not always straight, that is why automakers put steering wheels in cars. The following exercise will also help you to stay on course through the bends and detours. This could be negative events, negative people in day-to-day life, or past events that still have to be dealt with psychologically. In the left column write down a negative feeling or thought you have and in the right column write down how you would rather feel or think. This breaks the vicious cycle between conscious and subconscious with a positive. If you say "I am happy" the subconscious processes it and becomes happy. When the subconscious is happy it turns around and makes the conscious mind happy. A 'virtuous cycle' develops but it all starts with a conscious effort. Come back to these pages whenever you want to turn a negative thought or event into a positive one. This is as easy as turning a wheel.

I am sad.	I am happy.
I cannot afford it.	I am worth it.

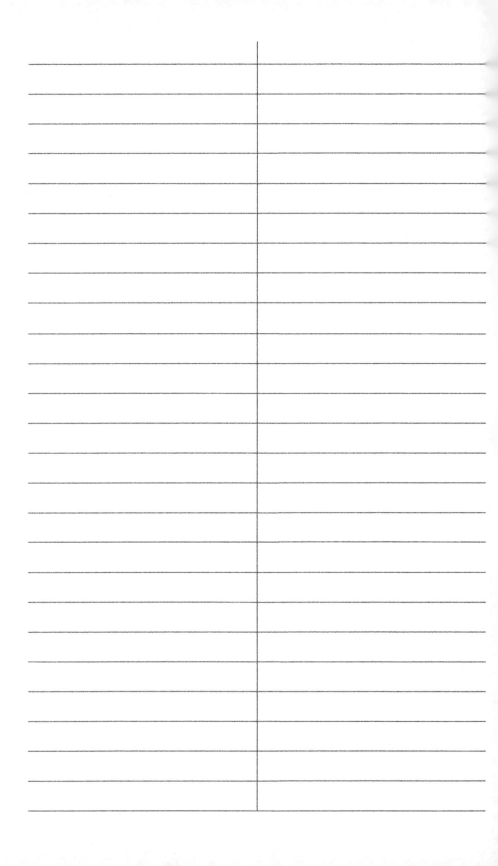

33 Days of Pure Gratitude

The mind can easily get bored if we keep doing the same things over and over again. If we are grateful for the same things every day the mind will go into autopilot as it becomes a chore.

It is important to find different things to be grateful for daily.

Gratitude is important because it directs our thoughts to look for the positive things in our lives, making us more positive in the process. It is an ordinary matter that brings about extraordinary results. Find new things every day that you can be grateful for. When you wake up in the morning you can be grateful for your bed, your breakfast or the job you go to every morning. You can be grateful for the salary and the opportunities that money affords you. Now it's your turn to extract the positives from your life and be grateful for it. Be creative.

---

gratitude

[grat-i-tood, -tyood] noun

the quality of being thankful; readiness to show appreciation for and to return kindness.

Today I am grateful for   Date:

1. _____

_____

2. _____

_____

3. _____

_____

Today I am grateful for   Date:

1. _____

_____

2. _____

_____

3. _____

_____

Today I am grateful for   Date:

1. _____

_____

2. _____

_____

3. _____

_____

Today I am grateful for   Date:

1.
_____

2.
_____

3.
_____

Today I am grateful for   Date:

1.
_____

2.
_____

3.
_____

Today I am grateful for   Date:

1.
_____

2.
_____

3.
_____

Today I am grateful for   Date:

1. _____

   _____

2. _____

   _____

3. _____

   _____

Today I am grateful for   Date:

1. _____

   _____

2. _____

   _____

3. _____

   _____

Today I am grateful for   Date:

1. _____

   _____

2. _____

   _____

3. _____

   _____

Today I am grateful for   Date:

1. _____

2. _____

3. _____

_____

Today I am grateful for   Date:

1. _____

2. _____

3. _____

_____

Today I am grateful for   Date:

1. _____

2. _____

3. _____

_____

Today I am grateful for   Date:

1. _____

_____

2. _____

_____

3. _____

_____

Today I am grateful for   Date:

1. _____

_____

2. _____

_____

3. _____

_____

Today I am grateful for   Date:

1. _____

_____

2. _____

_____

3. _____

_____

Today I am grateful for   Date:

1. _____

_____

2. _____

_____

3. _____

_____

Today I am grateful for   Date:

1. _____

_____

2. _____

_____

3. _____

_____

Today I am grateful for   Date:

1. _____

_____

2. _____

_____

3. _____

_____

Today I am grateful for   Date:

1. _____

2. _____

3. _____

Today I am grateful for   Date:

1. _____

2. _____

3. _____

Today I am grateful for   Date:

1. _____

2. _____

3. _____

Today I am grateful for   Date:

1.
_____

_____

2.
_____

_____

3.
_____

_____

Today I am grateful for   Date:

1.
_____

_____

2.
_____

_____

3.
_____

_____

Today I am grateful for   Date:

1.
_____

_____

2.
_____

_____

3.
_____

_____

Today I am grateful for   Date:

1. _____

_____

2. _____

_____

3. _____

_____

Today I am grateful for   Date:

1. _____

_____

2. _____

_____

3. _____

_____

Today I am grateful for   Date:

1. _____

_____

2. _____

_____

3. _____

_____

Today I am grateful for   Date:

1. _____

_____

2. _____

_____

3. _____

_____

Today I am grateful for   Date:

1. _____

_____

2. _____

_____

3. _____

_____

Today I am grateful for   Date:

1. _____

_____

2. _____

_____

3. _____

_____

Today I am grateful for   Date:

1. _____

_____

2. _____

_____

3. _____

_____

Today I am grateful for   Date:

1. _____

_____

2. _____

_____

3. _____

_____

Today I am grateful for   Date:

1. _____

_____

2. _____

_____

3. _____

_____

Ho'oponopono

This is the name of the ancient Hawaiian practice of forgiveness and reconciliation. It consists of four simple sentences:

1. I'm sorry.
2. Please forgive me.
3. I love you.
4. Thank you.

These sentences are important to say to anyone you would like to forgive or ask forgiveness from — including yourself. Yes, forgiveness is amazing because you can use it on yourself, too.

This forgiveness ritual is a crucial step in the healing process and to go through life with the ease of knowing that you do not have to keep carrying the baggage of your past.

Important Note: Forgive **Yourself First**. It does not matter for what, just do it. Release yourself from the shackles to which you have the keys to — then forgive everyone else.

With closed eyes and serene conviction, say the sentences above while thinking of the people you want to forgive. If forgiveness is a release from the shackles then just ask yourself, on whose account would you prefer to stay in a self-induced captivity — a captivity to which that person is most likely oblivious. The answer should be no one.

Reasons why you forgive yourself

People you forgive and the reasons for your forgiveness

Positive Affirmations

I deserve to be loved.

Money flows to me easily and effortlessly.

I believe in myself and the fact that I am successful.

I love my life

I AM A PRECIOUS PERSON WHO DESERVES TO BE RICH.

It does not matter where I am, I am surrounded by wealth.

This world is full of riches and there is plenty for all of us.

I am grateful for all the money that I have and will have.

There are no limits to my success.

I'm successful because I know what I want in life.

I live a fulfilled life.

My thoughts create my reality.

I can achieve anything I want.

I AM A GOOD ROLE MODEL.

I share my wealth and am rewarded with even more wealth.

Positive Affirmations

I can earn as much as I want.

Financial freedom makes me content.

Money is chasing me.

Every day offers me new possibilities to become richer.

I can achieve anything I put my mind to.

I LIVE IN A WORLD FULL OF OPULENCE.

Money always finds me.

Money flows naturally and effortlessly into my life.

xpect only good things in life and therefore get good things in life.

I live in abundance and prosperity.

I congratulate myself for my success.

I can earn as much as I want.

I am very thankful for my financial success.

My Financial Freedom makes me happy.

I AM GENEROUS TO MYSELF AND I AM GENEROUS TO OTHERS.

Everything is possible for me.

What makes you so special?

_____

_____

_____

_____

_____

_____

_____

_____

_____

_____

_____

_____

_____

_____

_____

_____

_____

_____

_____

_____

Habits

For better or worse, habits structure our lives. The outward appearance of a habit is an action done regularly without conscious effort. All actions start with thoughts, so the inward aspect of a habit would be the subconscious mind playing the same programmed thought over and over. That thought was formed either with intention or at random, by us or someone else. For the most part they were instilled into us by external factors in our most impressionable period — parents, teachers, siblings, etc., implant habits until the mind matures and is not as easily influenced, up until the age of seven.

Sometimes we do things a certain way and don't know why. The subconscious mind is where habits are anchored. Fortunately, there are two ways to unanchor them: through hypnosis and repetition. A hypnosis session can be very effective in changing thinking patterns and behaviors. When you go with repetition a habit tracker can help alter old habits and make new ones. All of our habits were learned so we can always learn new ones, even now. After all, we did not learn to drive a car in the womb, but rather by repetition. Just because a habit was established in the past does not establish its dominance in the future.

Repetition of positive affirmations for example, which are found throughout the book, is one of the most powerful ways to change negative thought cycles.

Repetition will lead to confidence. Being constantly reminded of your goals, with the aid of your vision boards, will lead to focus. Regular visualization, so real you can taste it, smell it, hear it and feel it, eliminates limiting beliefs. Writing down and tracking habits you want to establish develops habits with intention and purpose, replacing useless habits put there randomly. This completes the bridge between subconscious thought and action. This is fertile ground for success.

Write down only new and desired habits you want to track and thereby establish, not ones you want to eliminate.

Examples could be:

- Taking care of your eating habits and diet
- Acquire a new skill you need to be successful
- More exercise weekly
- Meditate every morning
- Devote time to reading books
- Better nutrition
- etc.

Write the habits you want to acquire in the sloping fields on the next page. Each time you have these new habits set, place an X in the box for that day. The more you repeat certain things, the faster they become habits. You now have one month to acquire new and beneficial habits.

Habit Tracker

Month _____

Year _____

Day												
1												
2												
3												
4												
5												
6												
7												
8												
9												
10												
11												
12												
13												
14												
15												
16												
17												
18												
19												
20												
21												
22												
23												
24												
25												
26												
27												
28												
29												
30												
31												

Your victories / What you are proud of

What makes you happy?

What gives you energy and motivation?

See The Positive

Too often we focus on the negative things in life. Of course, we shouldn't. No matter how bad a day gets, something positive can always be found to save it.

But if we let the positives pass and get too caught up in negative thoughts, this eventually will bring us into the wrong frequency. Like radio stations, we send and receive frequencies from our environment. If these frequencies are negative or if we are in the wrong "transmitter", then we are bound to attract discord and discontent, and misfortune seldom comes alone.

In the coming days you will learn to always see the positive in life and thereby radiate positive frequencies. Your task now is to write down only the positive things in your day for the next 33 days. No matter how bad a day has been, make sure that you find enough positive reasons why the day was still worthwhile. For example, if it rains the whole day you could write, "The plants have had enough water today and will blossom beautifully tomorrow."

Write down, in full sentences or point form, everything that gave you pleasure that day, even if it was just a delicious lunch or a message from a friend.

Naturally, you'll take your notes in the evenings so that you go to sleep on a positive note and wake up in a positive vibration the next morning.

"You always have a free choice,
but you are never free from the
consequences of your choice."

So choose now, to always see the <u>positive</u> in everything!

What was good today?   Date:

_____

_____

_____

_____

_____

_____

What was good today?   Date:

_____

_____

_____

_____

_____

_____

What was good today?   Date:

_____

_____

_____

_____

_____

What was good today?   Date:

_____
_____
_____
_____
_____
_____

What was good today?   Date:

_____
_____
_____
_____
_____
_____

What was good today?   Date:

_____
_____
_____
_____
_____
_____

What was good today?   Date:

_____

_____

_____

_____

_____

_____

What was good today?   Date:

_____

_____

_____

_____

_____

_____

What was good today?   Date:

_____

_____

_____

_____

_____

What was good today?   Date:

_____
_____
_____
_____
_____
_____

What was good today?   Date:

_____
_____
_____
_____
_____

What was good today?   Date:

_____
_____
_____
_____
_____

What was good today?   Date:

_____

_____

_____

_____

_____

_____

What was good today?   Date:

_____

_____

_____

_____

_____

What was good today?   Date:

_____

_____

_____

_____

_____

What was good today?   Date:

_____

_____

_____

_____

_____

_____

What was good today?   Date:

_____

_____

_____

_____

_____

_____

What was good today?   Date:

_____

_____

_____

_____

_____

_____

What was good today?   Date:

_____

_____

_____

_____

_____

_____

What was good today?   Date:

_____

_____

_____

_____

_____

_____

What was good today?   Date:

_____

_____

_____

_____

_____

_____

What was good today?   Date:

_____
_____
_____
_____
_____
_____

What was good today?   Date:

_____
_____
_____
_____
_____
_____

What was good today?   Date:

_____
_____
_____
_____
_____
_____

What was good today?   Date:

_____

_____

_____

_____

_____

What was good today?   Date:

_____

_____

_____

_____

_____

What was good today?   Date:

_____

_____

_____

_____

_____

What was good today?   Date:

_____

_____

_____

_____

_____

_____

What was good today?   Date:

_____

_____

_____

_____

_____

_____

What was good today?   Date:

_____

_____

_____

_____

_____

_____

What was good today?   Date:

_____

_____

_____

_____

_____

_____

What was good today?   Date:

_____

_____

_____

_____

_____

_____

What was good today?   Date:

_____

_____

_____

_____

_____

_____

Vocabulary

Some words and phrases should be deleted from your vocabulary because they lead you into a negative feedback loop of thoughts which definitely do not help you:

"I WISH..."

Example: I wish I was more self-confident.
Instead: I choose to be more self-confident.

"...NEVER..."

Example: I will never be successful in life.
Instead: I am always successful.

"I CAN'T..."

Example: I cannot do this.
Instead: I decide to do it. I can.

"...HOPE..."

Example: I hope I get a raise.
Instead: I will do my best to get a raise.

"IF..."

Example: If my contract gets extended, I will go to restaurant XYZ.
Instead: I am always worth going to that restaurant, no matter the circumstances.

"...TRY..."

Trying implies failure. Either you <u>do</u> or <u>do not</u>.

Remember: What comes out of your mouth comes into your life.

Words and phrases you use that need rewording

Focus Wheel

This focus wheel - inspired by Abraham Hicks and Doug Graham - is here to help you so you can easily and effortlessly focus on your desires in any area of life, be it relationships, wealth, health, etc. Simply write in the middle of the wheel your main intention/goal and add related empowering positive sentences around it.

- Always word your desire/intention in a positive way, never from a place of lack. Instead of saying, for example, "I want to lose 10 pounds," say "I love the thought of having the body I want."
- Write sentences around the circle that are related to the positive FEELINGS associated with your main desire. Start with "I love the feeling of...," or "I love the thought of...," or "It feels great to...," etc.
- The surrounding sentences do not necessarily have to do with the desire/intention in the middle. You can write anything that expresses good feelings and emotions. You can write "I love listening to the birds in the morning," or "I love watching cute little baby animals." The most important part is that you write down sentences that raise your vibration and bring you to a very happy state of FEELING.
- Read the sentence in the circle first and then read each surrounding sentences two to three times back to back in order to get into that FEELING state. Really get into it, jump or move around with joy, breathe deeply, smile and raise your energy, while turning your wheel and reading the sentences.
- Come back to the circle often to anchor your positive vibes on your main goal.
- Alternatively you can turn on happy music and move with it while reading the sentences and getting in tune with your desires.
- Do this exercise for at least one to two minutes, several times a day. You can start with it early in the morning to set the vibration for the day, or before bed to set the vibration for your rest.
- Remember to keep it a realistic goal, otherwise a goal too lofty (i. e. a million dollars) would introduce fear or doubt and thereby disrupting the positive vibrations.

Focus Wheel - Example

The thought of money coming my way makes me feel amazing

I love the feeling of extra money coming in

I know what it feels like to be blessed with additional income

I love the feeling of doing good things with my money

I love sharing with others

I love the freedom that my extra income provides me

It feels awesome seeing my bank account grow

I love the feeling of circulating my extra income on whatever I want

I love the thought of having unlimited abundance

I love the thought of being, doing and having whatever I want

I can't wait to manifest even more extra income

Receiving extra money makes me feel very very happy

I love having an extra $1000 in my life

Intention set on (date): _____

Manifested on (date): _____

Other good things that came with my manifestation: _____

_____

_____

Focus Wheel

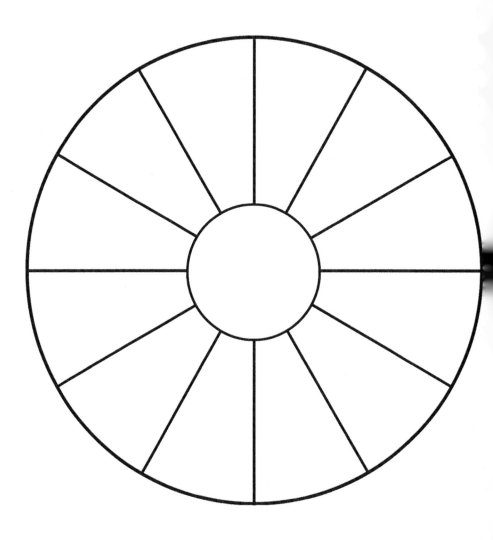

Intention set on (date): _____

Manifested on (date): _____

Other good things that came with my manifestation: _____

_____

_____

Nothing Comes From Nothing

In order to achieve anything in life we have to take action to get the ball rolling. We cannot expect to meet our dream partner, for example, if we sit at home all day long. We have to step out of the house to even have a chance of finding someone.

For the next 15 days, write down exactly what you have done to achieve your goals and come closer to your dreams — short and long term.

You do not have to write the whole process, only the important things. The rest will come.

Date:

What I have accomplished today to achieve my goals

_____

_____

_____

_____

_____

_____

_____

Date:

What I have accomplished today to achieve my goals

_____

_____

_____

_____

_____

_____

_____

Date:

What I have accomplished today to achieve my goals

_____

_____

_____

_____

_____

_____

_____

Date:

What I have accomplished today to achieve my goals

_____

_____

_____

_____

_____

_____

_____

_____

Date:

What I have accomplished today to achieve my goals

_____

_____

_____

_____

_____

_____

_____

_____

Date:

What I have accomplished today to achieve my goals

_____

_____

_____

_____

_____

_____

_____

Date:

What I have accomplished today to achieve my goals

_____

_____

_____

_____

_____

_____

_____

_____

Date:

What I have accomplished today to achieve my goals

_____

_____

_____

_____

_____

_____

_____

_____

Date:

What I have accomplished today to achieve my goals

_____

_____

_____

_____

_____

_____

_____

_____

Date:

What I have accomplished today to achieve my goals

_____

_____

_____

_____

_____

_____

_____

Date:

What I have accomplished today to achieve my goals

_____

_____

_____

_____

_____

_____

_____

Date:

What I have accomplished today to achieve my goals

_____

_____

_____

_____

_____

_____

_____

_____

Date:

What I have accomplished today to achieve my goals

_____

_____

_____

_____

_____

_____

_____

_____

Date:

What I have accomplished today to achieve my goals

_____

_____

_____

_____

_____

_____

_____

_____

Date:

What I have accomplished today to achieve my goals

_____

_____

_____

_____

_____

_____

_____

_____

_____

List of what you have manifested so far in your life

_____

_____

_____

_____

_____

_____

_____

_____

_____

_____

_____

_____

_____

_____

_____

_____

_____

_____

_____

_____

_____

Areas to improve

Seek! And ye shall find.

```
F  U  N  G  I  B  L  K  H  C  B  L  I  S  S
R  J  U  P  D  I  S  I  A  P  G  V  S  P  T
E  H  X  D  G  P  G  E  P  O  W  E  R  G  O
E  N  D  H  L  O  A  R  P  H  S  X  Z  E  N
D  R  T  F  L  S  U  M  I  N  D  F  U  L  V
O  V  I  R  E  I  C  O  N  K  H  L  F  V  E
M  J  B  Q  G  T  V  L  E  N  E  R  G  Y  B
T  T  H  T  F  I  G  W  S  M  N  S  C  M  E
M  C  R  I  S  V  E  C  S  A  K  X  H  U  L
E  M  K  U  O  E  H  R  E  U  D  G  A  N  I
C  A  S  E  S  N  M  F  R  E  C  D  N  U  F
O  H  H  R  Q  T  G  E  K  S  V  C  G  E  E
N  C  E  T  L  N  A  U  D  B  P  M  E  H  K
T  E  S  E  M  O  B  J  A  I  R  A  B  S  R
E  B  C  A  R  V  V  P  M  K  T  F  S  R  S
N  J  R  E  L  A  X  E  D  S  L  A  X  S  F
T  F  S  E  L  I  P  R  E  S  E  N  T  C  T
N  C  O  U  R  A  G  E  L  J  O  Y  E  E  W
```

POSITIVE HAPPINESS ZEN LIGHT FREEDOM
MINDFUL RELAXED ENERGY SUCCESS GIFT LIFE
BLISS TRUST CONTENT MEDITATE FUN COURAGE
LOVE POWER CHEER JOY PRESENT CHANGE

CHECK OUT OTHER BOOKS BY AGRIM RANGANATHAN ON AMAZON!

THE BOOKLET "MANIFESTATION TOOLS" INCLUDES BUSINESS CARDS, BOARDING PASSES, CHECKS AND MORE; IT HELPS YOU VISUALIZE BETTER AND TO FEEL WHAT IT IS REALLY LIKE TO HOLD YOUR DREAMS AND DESIRES IN YOUR HANDS.

NO MORE SIFTING THROUGH MAGAZINES!!!

IN THIS BOOKLET YOU WILL FIND PICTURES AND WORD ART QUOTES FOR ALL AREAS OF LIFE:
- HEALTH & FITNESS
- WELL-BEING
- PERSONAL DEVELOPMENT
- FAMILY & FRIENDS
- FINANCES & MONEY
- SUCCESS & CAREER
- LOVE & RELATIONSHIPS
- FUN & RECREATION
- TRAVEL & ADVENTURE
- SPIRITUALITY
- AND MORE...

VISION BOARDS IN BOOK FORM

WOULD YOU RATHER HAVE A VISION BOARD THAT YOU CAN CARRY AROUND? YOU DON'T WANT ANYONE TO LOOK AT THE VISION BOARD ON YOUR WALL BUT RATHER KEEP IT PRIVATE? THEN THIS VISION BOARD IN BOOK FORM IS RIGHT FOR YOU!

THE PAGES ARE HALF EMPTY AND HALF RULED, SO YOU CAN PASTE PICTURES OR DRAW IN THE EMPTY AREAS AND PUT INTO WORDS WHAT YOU WANT TO ACCOMPLISH.

THERE IS ENOUGH ROOM TO ALSO ADD AFFIRMATIONS.

Disclaimer

This book serves as an aid to self-help. Agrim Ranganathan can not guarantee success and is not responsible for the individual success — or lack thereof — of the users of these techniques. Everyone has different life circumstances, different goals and different approaches. Every person's success story is individual and unique. Agrim has consumed and tried a lot on the subject. These techniques have helped Agrim transform his life. He has put these techniques together to help readers like you reach and manifest your goals.

This work, with all its contents, is protected by copyright. Any use outside the copyright law is not permitted without consent. This applies in particular to reproductions, translations, processing and public and electronic accessibility.

If you have questions or comments feel free to email sd.international.inc@gmail.com

Did you like this book? Please consider leaving a review or rating on Amazon.   ★★★★★

Spread the word and help Agrim help others as well.

Thank you and happy manifesting!

Printed in Great Britain
by Amazon

23681858R00064